Sherilin Chanek
Illustrations by Cameron Eagle

I'm a rock. I've been around.

I may not be the oldest rock you will ever see, but I am older than you and your grandparents, and their grandparents, too. Over the years my size and shape have changed many times. Sometimes I change so much that I hardly know myself.

Before I was a rock I was hot stuff. Really.

Hot, melted rock inside the earth is called *magma* (MAG-muh).

Magma

A long, long time ago I was part of a huge sheet of melted rock deep under the ground. It was very hot there, inside the earth.

One day, the melted rock pushed up inside a mountain. It pushed harder until the mountain blew its top. The mountain that exploded was called a *volcano*. From that volcano I was blown out into the world.

Lava (LAH-vuh) is magma that comes out of the ground.

Once I was out, I started to change. As I got cooler, I also got harder. Soon I was a solid rock.

Hot!

Cooler!

Solid!

In those days I was much larger and heavier than I am today. There were many other rocks around me. I wasn't the biggest or the smallest—I was a nice size, and good-looking too, if I say so myself.

Igneous (IG-nee-us) rocks form when magma or lava cools.

Then I sat around for a long, long time. What do you think I did all that time?

You're right. Not much. I am a rock. However, I did see many changes around me. I saw dinosaurs come and go. I saw seeds grow into trees. In fact, I have seen the tallest, thickest trees that have ever lived. I have also seen the tiniest of bugs come and go.

I saw the sun beat down its hottest. I saw the wind blow its fastest. I saw the rain fall its hardest. Each year was different from the next.

I changed too. The sun made me hotter and hotter during the day, and then at night I cooled down suddenly. I cracked, and pieces fell off me.

The wind and rain rubbed and thumped me so much that they wore tiny pieces off me, too. All these things slowly made me smaller and smaller.

One day the earth under me shook. I rolled and rolled down the hill. I couldn't stop myself and I hit other rocks on the way down. We all broke into smaller pieces.

Then I rolled into a river. The water pushed me along because I wasn't very heavy anymore. Sometimes I got stuck in the mud. All that time I kept changing. The water kept rubbing tiny pieces off me. It made me smaller and smoother.

The river pushed me down to the sea, where I sank to the bottom.

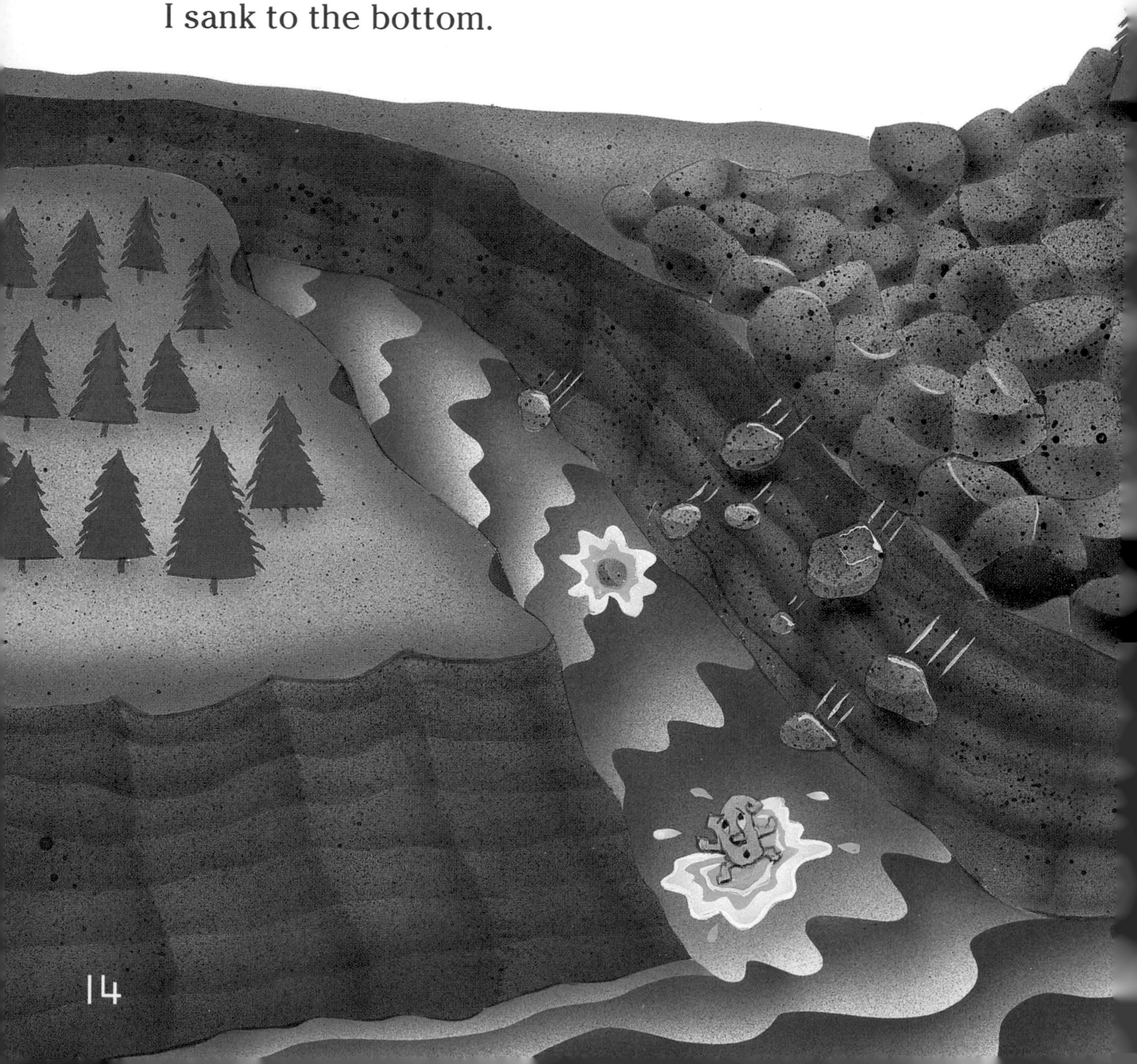

Rocks and soil are carried by rivers to the sea, where they sink to the bottom as *sediment* (SED-uh-ment).

Over the years, mud and other rocks piled on top of me. I sat there under the layers.

More heavy rocks and more heavy mud piled on top of me. They pushed me down more and more. Over many, many years, I started to stick to other rocks. After a very long time, I became a new rock made up of pieces of older rocks. I became big and heavy again.

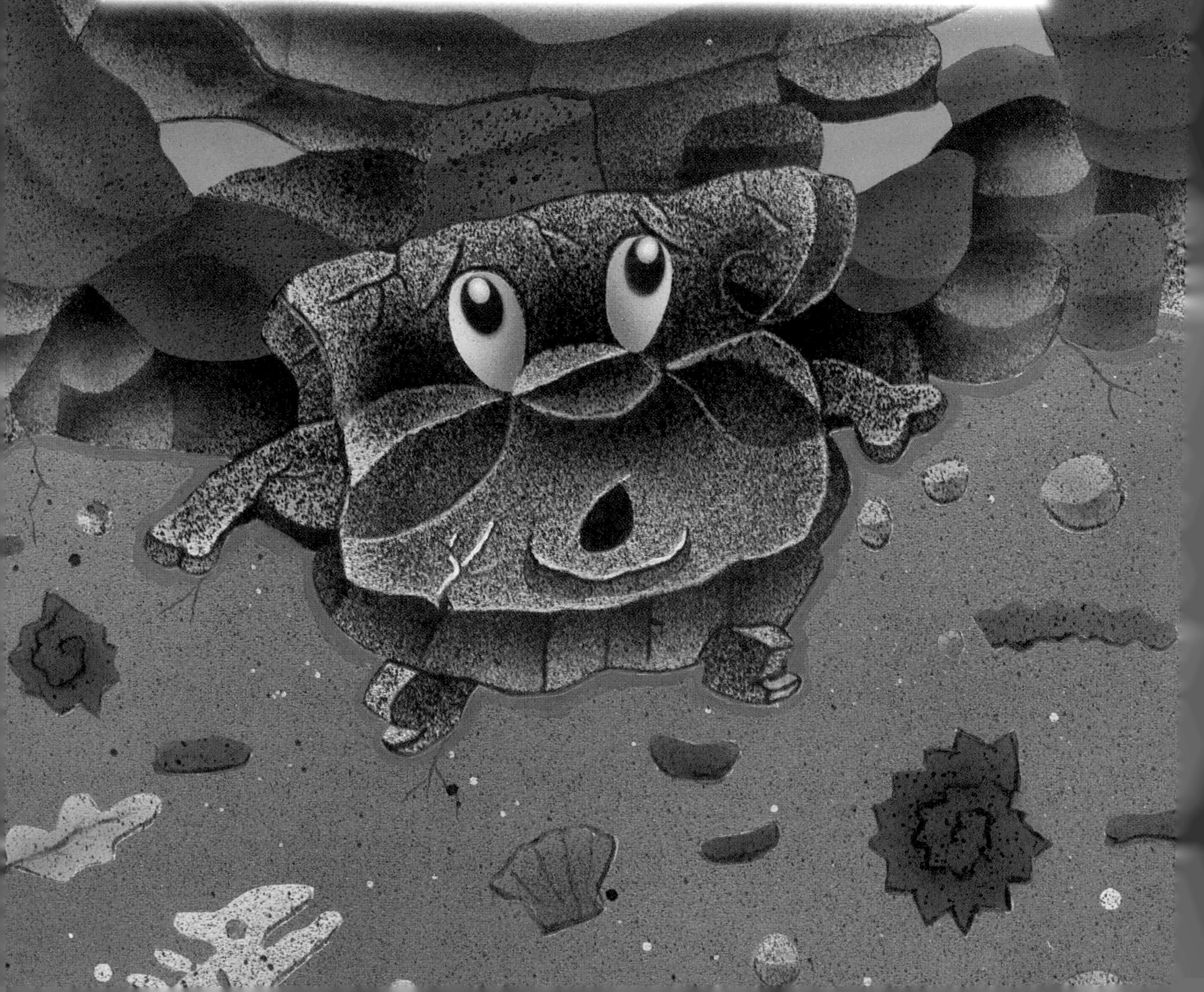

Sedimentary (sed-uh-MEN-tar-ee) rocks form when layers of broken-up rock settle and harden.

Many, many years passed. I got buried even deeper, and I got hotter and hotter. I could feel myself change again.

Now I was a different rock. The heat and heavy stuff had changed me. Now I had wavy stripes. I was even fancier than before. In fact, I was the fanciest I could get.

Heavy layers and extreme heat change igneous and sedimentary rocks into *metamorphic* (met-uh-MORE-fik) rocks. An agate is one kind of metamorphic rock.

After a long, long time I started to change yet again. I sank lower and lower into the earth. The deeper I went, the hotter I became. Then I started to melt. Once again I became part of the melted rock deep inside the earth. I was in the deepest place I could be. I was magma again. Then my story started all over again.

People call my story the "rock cycle." A cycle is like a circle because it doesn't have an end.

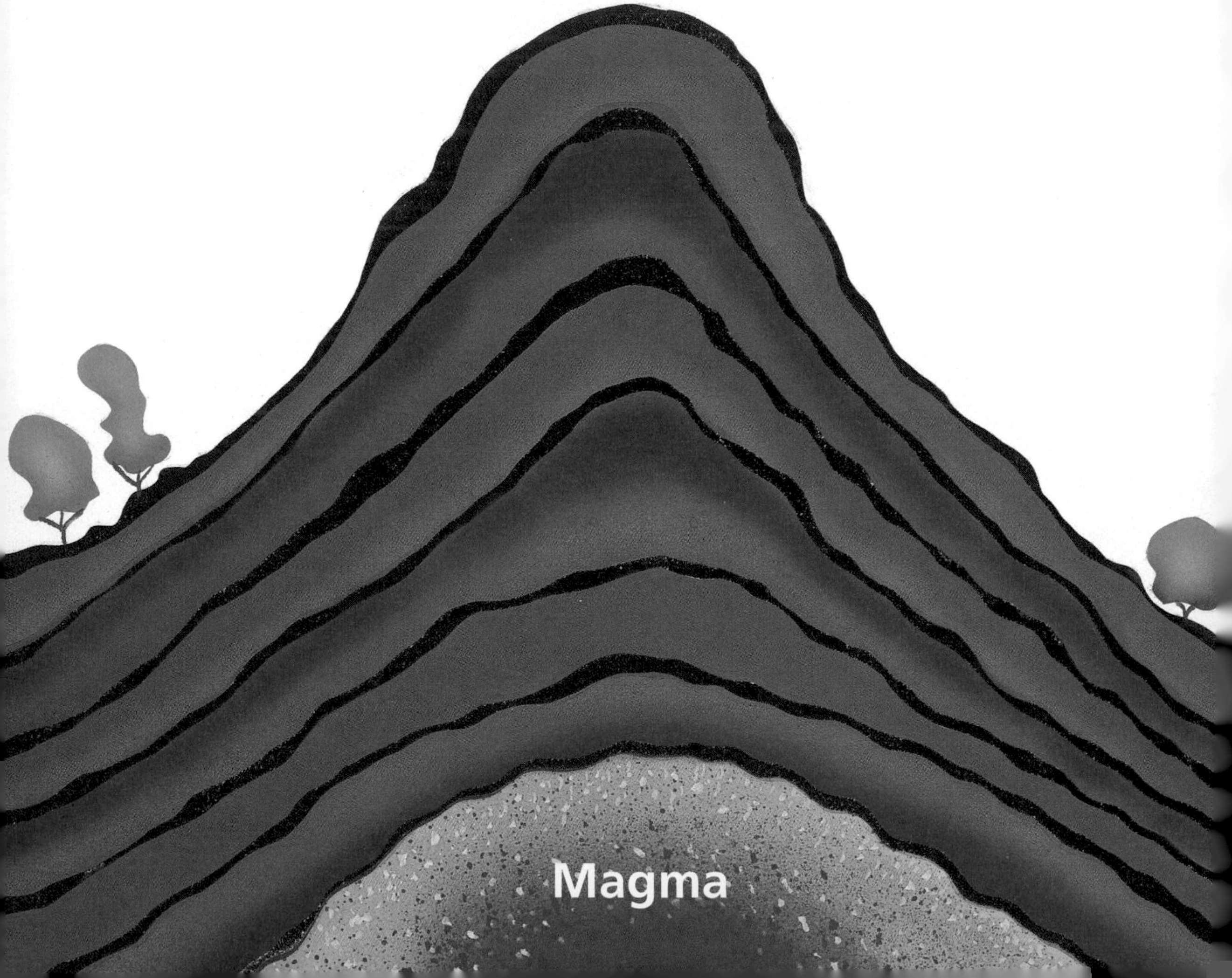

Magma

The Rock Cycle

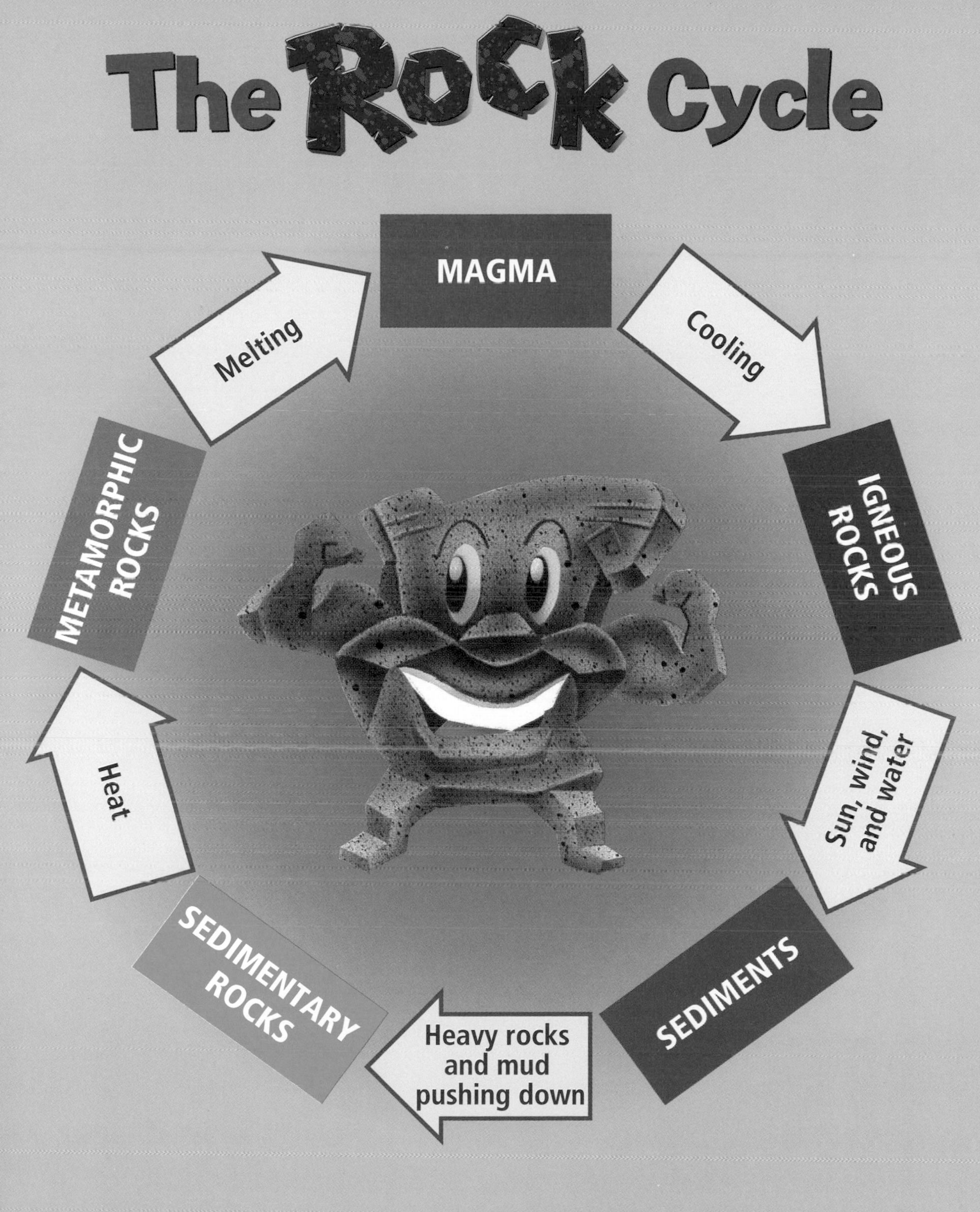

Today I sit in a box of rocks kept by a boy named Tony. It's not the nicest place I have ever been, but I keep myself entertained. I get along with the other rocks, and I like Tony, too.

One day Tony's friend asked him, "Why do you collect those boring rocks? They all look the same to me." That made Tony angry. It made me even angrier.

All rocks face the same changes, and we face the same cycles, but not all rocks are the same. Some rocks are softer than I am. Some are harder. Some are rounder. Some are flatter. Some are bigger. Some are smaller. Some are lighter. Some are heavier. We are made of different things and we come from different places.

How can we be boring? We are the oldest things on earth.

Tony knows it. You know it. I know it, too.

I'm a rock. I've been around.

THINK ABOUT IT

1. In your own words, describe how the rock in the story changed.
2. Do you think the rocks in your playground will ever change? Why or why not?
3. How have you changed in the past five years?